Basics

Flattened crimp

1 Hold the crimp bead using the tip of your chainnose pliers. Squeeze the pliers firmly to flatten the crimp.

2 Tug the clasp to make sure the crimp has a solid grip on the wire. If the wire slides, remove the crimp bead and repeat the steps with a new crimp bead.

Folded crimp

1 Position the crimp bead in the notch closest to the crimping pliers' handle.

2 Separate the wires and firmly squeeze the crimp.

3 Move the crimp into the notch at the pliers' tip and hold the crimp as shown. Squeeze the crimp bead, folding it in half at the indentation.

4 Test that the folded crimp is secure.

Plain loops

1 Trim the wire ⅜ in. (1cm) above the top bead. Make a right angle bend close to the bead.

2 Grab the wire's tip with roundnose pliers. Roll the wire to form a half circle. Release the wire.

3 Reposition the pliers in the loop and continue rolling.

4 The finished loop should form a centered circle above the bead.

Wrapped loops

1 Make sure you have at least 1¼ in. (3.2cm) of wire above the bead. With the tip of your chainnose pliers, grasp the wire directly above the bead. Bend the wire (above the pliers) into a right angle.

2 Using roundnose pliers, position the jaws in the bend.

3 Bring the wire over the top jaw of the roundnose pliers.

4 Reposition the pliers' lower jaw snugly into the loop. Curve the wire downward around the bottom of the roundnose pliers. This is the first half of a wrapped loop.

5 Position the chainnose pliers' jaws across the loop.

6 Wrap the wire around the wire stem, covering the stem between the loop and the top of the bead. Trim the excess wire and press the cut end close to the wraps with chainnose pliers.

Opening and closing loops and jump rings

1 Hold a jump ring or plain loop with two pairs of chainnose pliers or chainnose and roundnose pliers, as shown.

2 To open the loop or jump ring, bring the tips of one pair of pliers toward you and push the tips of the other pair away from you.

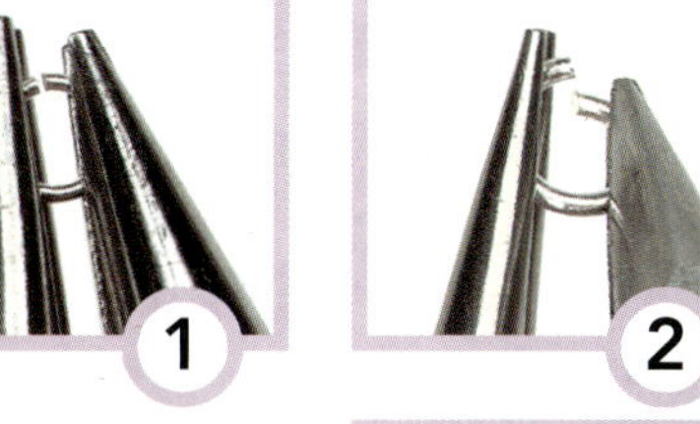

3 Reverse the steps to close the open loop or ring.

Surgeon's knot

Cross the right end over the left end and go through the loop. Go over and through again. Cross the left end over the right end and go through once. Pull the ends to tighten.

Classic strung necklace

For hundreds of years, the art of beadmaking has been a proud tradition in Venice. The Venetian glass beads featured in this easy necklace are an updated take on a traditional form. Using seed beads and spacers allows the beautiful raspberry and champagne hues of the beads to shine in this modern interpretation of a timeless classic.

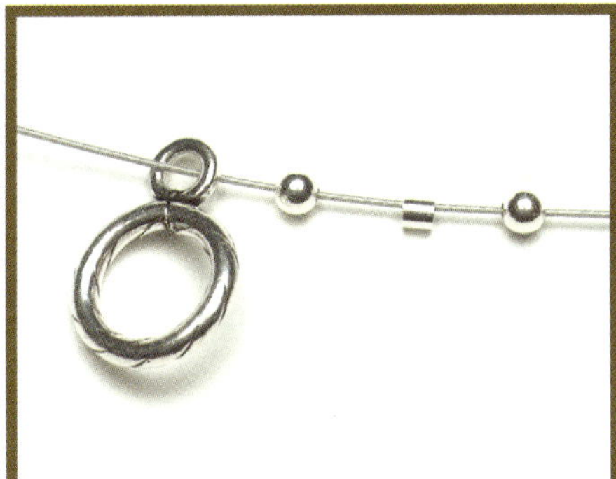

necklace • 1. For an 18-in. (46cm) necklace, cut a 24-in. (61cm) length of beading wire. String a round silver bead, a crimp bead, another round, and the loop end of the toggle clasp. If the hole in your round bead is too narrow for a wire to pass through twice, insert the tip of a roundnose pliers into the hole and twist gently to enlarge it.

2. Go back through these beads and tighten the wire so it forms a small loop around the clasp. Crimp the crimp bead (Basics, p. 3) and trim the excess wire.

3. String a seed bead, a bead cap, a Venetian bead, and another bead cap. The open end of each bead cap should face the square.

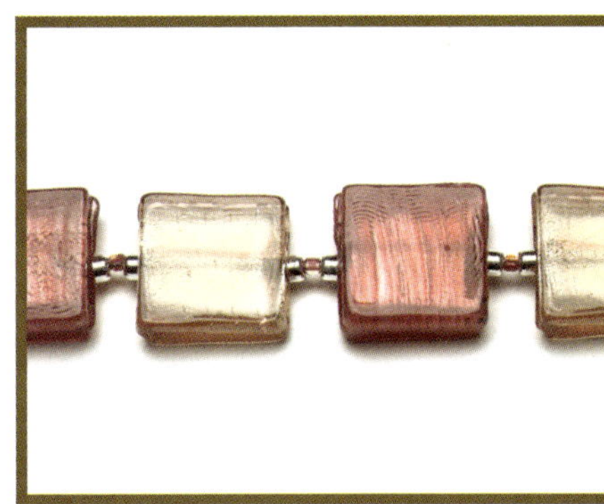

4. Continue stringing this pattern, alternating between raspberry- and champagne-colored squares. Use all 18 squares. End with a bead cap.

5. String a seed bead, a round bead, a crimp bead, another round, and the toggle end of the clasp. Lay the necklace in a circular shape before crimping to make sure it has enough flexibility.

6. Repeat step 2 to finish the clasp.

– Susan Holland
Visit Susan's Web site, venetianbeads.com.

Supply List

both projects

- 5g Japanese seed beads, size 10º or 11º (raspberry)
- flexible beading wire, .018 or .019
- chainnose pliers or crimping tool
- diagonal wire cutters
- roundnose pliers (optional)

necklace

- **9** 20mm square Venetian glass beads (Rubino Platino)
- **9** 20mm square Venetian glass beads (Champagne Pink)
- **36** bead caps
- **4** 3mm round silver beads
- toggle clasp
- **2** crimp beads

bracelet

- **4** 20mm square Venetian glass beads (Rubino Platino)
- **3** 20mm square Venetian glass beads (Champagne Pink)
- **14** bead caps
- **4** 3mm round silver beads
- toggle clasp
- **2** crimp beads

bracelet • Measure your wrist and add 5 in. (13cm) for finishing. Cut a piece of wire to that length. Follow the necklace instructions to string the bracelet and attach the clasp. ✤

Marine necklace

Large, flat Peruvian opals are luxuriantly smooth and comfortable against the skin. Handmade Thai silver sea creatures complement the highly polished stones. Choosing beads and stones of the same thickness helps the finished piece lie flat around your neck. This necklace is versatile—sporty enough for daytime attire and sophisticated enough for evening wear.

1. For an 18-in. (46cm) necklace, cut a 24-in. (61cm) piece of beading wire. Center the focal bead on the wire and string two 4mm beads and a spacer on each side. Tape one end.

2. String a flat gemstone nugget, two spacers, a large accent bead, two spacers, and another nugget.

3. String a spacer, a 4mm bead, a spacer, and the smaller accent bead. Repeat. End with a spacer, a 4mm bead, and a spacer.

4. String a flat gemstone nugget and a spacer. Tape the end. Repeat steps 2 through 4 on the other end of the necklace. Check the fit and add or remove beads on each side, if necessary.

5. String a large-hole silver bead, a crimp bead, a round spacer, and the hook end of the clasp (see p. 7 sidebar). Go back through these beads, tighten the wire, and make a folded crimp (Basics, p. 3). Don't trim the excess wire.

6. Slide the wire tail through the large-hole bead. Slide all the beads toward the clasp and maneuver the crimp inside the large-hole bead. The large hole should be flush against the round bead. Trim the excess wire.

7. At the other end of the necklace, remove the tape and string a crimp bead. Go back through the crimp and the spacer, leaving a ¾-in. (2cm) loop.

8. Slide the crimp and spacer toward the gemstone and crimp the crimp bead. Cut a 4-in. (10cm) piece of beading wire, pass it through the loop, and fold it in half.

9. String a large-hole bead and 2.5mm round spacer over both ends of the 4-in. wire. Slide both beads over the two loops, covering the crimp with the large-hole bead. Slide the spacer against it. A small loop of beading wire will extend beyond the spacer. Remove the 4-in. piece of wire.

10. Open the clasp loop and attach it to the loop of beading wire. Close the clasp loop. If your clasp doesn't have a loop that opens, attach a split ring to the beading wire. Trim the excess wire.

– Erica Morris
Contact Erica at PO Box 1296, Moreno Valley, CA 92556-1296.

SupplyList

necklace

- large silver focal bead (Tiger Tiger, 510-236-9917, tiger-tiger.com)
- **6-8** flat Peruvian opal nuggets, approximately 20 x 30mm (770-696-5321, ebeadshop.com)
- **10-12** 4mm round Peruvian opals
- **2** silver accent beads, approximately 14 x 28mm
- **4** silver accent beads, approximately 10 x 15mm
- **2** 10mm large-hole silver beads
- **2** 2.5mm round spacer beads
- **8** 7mm flat spacer beads
- **16-20** 3mm flat spacer beads
- flexible beading wire, .024
- hook-and-eye clasp (or custom clasp, see below)
- split ring (optional)
- chainnose and crimping pliers
- diagonal wire cutters

custom clasp (optional)

- 10mm silver accent bead
- **2** 3mm round spacer beads
- 7 in. (18cm) 18- or 20-gauge sterling silver wire
- chainnose and roundnose pliers
- diagonal wire cutters

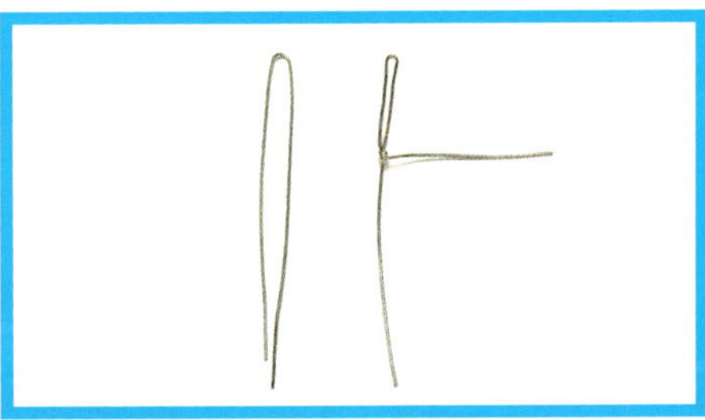

custom clasp

1. Cut a 7-in. (18cm) length of 18- or 20-gauge wire and bend it in half.

2. Cross half the wire over the other about 1½ in. (4cm) below the fold. Wrap the bent piece around the straight wire twice. Trim the wire close to the wraps.

3. String a spacer, an accent bead, and a spacer on the straight wire. Make a wrapped loop (Basics) below the spacer and trim the tail. Pinch the wires together above the accent bead with chainnose pliers. Make a slight bend at the tip of the fold.

4. Use roundnose pliers to curve the loop downward, making sure the bent tip faces outward as shown. ✤

Twisted pearl necklace

Freshwater pearls are beautiful and classic. In a teardrop shape, they convey a touch of whimsy. When strung, these pearls fan out on each side, giving the finished necklace an irregular line. Twisting two strands together enhances this effect. For extra sparkle and shine, string your necklace with Swarovski crystals interspersed at random intervals.

SupplyList

- **2** 16-in. (41cm) strands side-drilled teardrop pearls
- **20** 6-8mm round Swarovski crystals
- flexible beading wire, .014 or .015
- **8** 3mm round beads
- **4** crimp beads
- 2-strand clasp
- chainnose or crimping pliers
- diagonal wire cutters

1. Determine the finished length of your necklace (This one is 18 in./46cm), add 6 in. (15cm), and cut two pieces of beading wire to that length.

String a crimp bead and a 3mm bead and go through one of the clasp's loops. Go back through the beads, tighten the wire to form a small loop around the clasp, and crimp the crimp bead (Basics, p. 3). Repeat to attach the second wire to the available clasp loop.

When stringing a necklace that's meant to be worn with a twist, allow an extra inch or two (2.5-5cm) in length because twisting the strands shortens them.

2. String a 3mm bead on each wire, sliding it over the wire tail. Trim the excess wire. Then string the pearls, adding 10 randomly spaced crystals to each strand. Continue until each strand is about ½ in. (1.3cm) short of the finished length.

3. If your clasp is open, close it so you can attach the strands easily without twisting them. Working with the upper strand, string a 3mm bead, a crimp bead, and a 3mm bead and go through the clasp's upper loop. Go back through the last three beads, tighten the wire as before, and check the pearls to make sure no wire shows along the strand. Crimp the crimp bead. Trim the excess wire.

4. Attach the remaining strand to the lower clasp loop, as in step 3. Give the strands a twist when you put on the necklace. ✤

– by Anne Nikolai Kloss
Contact Anne at annekloss@mac.com.

Multistrand bracelet

Stringing a six-strand bracelet is easier than you think. Whether it's composed of beads in the same shape and color or beads in a variety of shapes and a rainbow of colors, you'll want to make one for every occasion.

1. Determine the finished length of your bracelet (this one is 7 in./18cm), add 5 in. (13cm), and cut six strands of beading wire to this length. String an alternating pattern of 8mm beads and seed beads on each strand, leaving enough wire for finishing. Begin and end each strand with an 8mm bead.

SupplyList

- 2 16-in. (41cm) strands 8mm oval fiber optic glass beads
- 10g size 11º Japanese seed beads
- 6 crimp beads
- 3-strand slide clasp
- flexible beading wire, .014 or .015
- chainnose or crimping pliers
- diagonal wire cutter

2. String two seed beads onto each beading wire. String one crimp bead and one seed bead over two wires.

3. String both wires through a clasp loop. Go back through the seed bead and crimp bead. Separate the strands and go through the next two seed beads. Crimp the crimp bead (Basics, p. 3). Trim the excess wire.

Repeat steps 2 and 3 to finish the remaining strands. Before attaching the other half of the clasp, be sure to position it opposite the first half. Avoid twisting or crossing the strands. ✤

– Paulette Biedenbender
Contact Paulette at h8winters@sbcglobal.net.

Double-strand necklace

A triangular stone pendant highlights a two-strand necklace for a retro look that's perfect with today's fashions. Whether your style is earthy and ethnic or summer casual, this necklace can be made to suit you.

The agate necklace measures 20 in. (51cm). For balance, keep the pendant size in mind when determining a suitable length for the finished necklace.

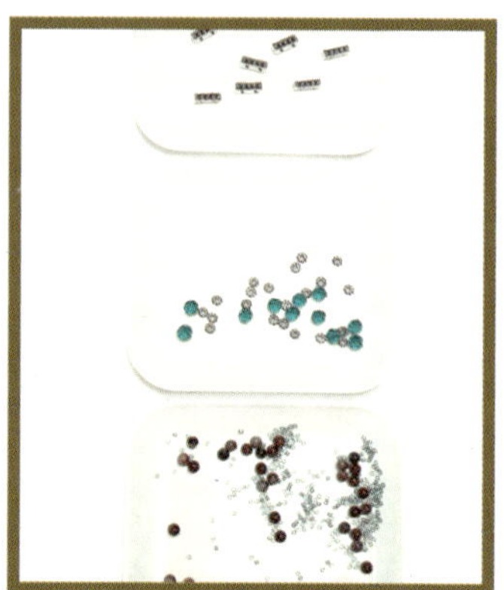

1. Pour your beads onto a few trays to save time when you string. Determine the finished length for your necklace, add 6 in. (15cm), and cut two pieces of Fireline to that length. Thread a needle on each end of both strands. Set one strand aside.

2. Center the pendant on one strand of Fireline. Thread enough seed beads to form a loose ring around the top of the pendant.

3. String both needles through a 4mm bead, seed bead, 4mm bead, seed bead, 4mm bead, and spacer.

4. Repeat these steps with the remaining strand of Fireline so you have two identical bead sequences attached to the pendant.

String a two-holed bead or spacer bar as shown. If your two-holed beads have different front and back sides, lay the piece flat to help you string them correctly.

5. Using both needles on one side, string a spacer, 4mm bead, seed bead, 4mm bead, spacer, 6mm bead, and another spacer.

6. Separate the two strands and string three seed beads on each.

7. On one of these strands, string a 4mm bead, seed bead, 4mm bead, spacer, 6mm bead, spacer, 4mm bead, seed bead, and 4mm bead.

8. String the pattern on the adjacent strand, then string a two-holed bead.

9. Repeat steps 7 and 8 four or more times, until you are 2 in. (5cm) short of half the desired length. To string the other side of the necklace, repeat steps 5 through 9.

10. On one strand, string the pattern in step 7, then three seed beads. Repeat on the adjacent strand.

11. String both strands through a spacer, 6mm bead, spacer, 4mm bead, seed bead, and bead tip.

Supply List

both necklaces

- **2** clamshell bead tips
- **2** 5mm split rings
- toggle clasp
- Fireline fishing line, 8-lb. test
- **4** beading needles, #10
- G-S Hypo Cement
- chainnose or roundnose pliers
- split ring pliers
- small trays or dishes

yellow jade necklace

- axe-shaped pendant drilled front to back, yellow jade
- **2** 16-in. (41cm) strands 4mm round yellow quartz beads
- 16-in. strand 6mm round sponge coral beads
- **13** 12 x 18mm 2-holed sponge coral beads
- 10g seed beads, size 14º, reddish brown
- **68** 4mm gold spacers

brown agate necklace

- triangular pendant drilled front to back, agate (Fire Mountain Gems, 800-355-2137)
- **2** 16-in. (41cm) strands 4mm round jasper beads
- **32** 6mm round Swarovski crystals, indicolite
- **11** 4 x 11mm 2-holed silver spacer bars
- 10g Delicas, silvery blue
- **60** 3mm silver spacers

12. On one strand, string a seed bead. Tie a surgeon's knot (Basics, p. 3) around the bead. Glue the knot and trim the ends to ⅛ in. (3mm). Gently close the bead tip using chainnose pliers or your fingers. Repeat steps 10 through 12 on the other side of the necklace.

13. Attach a split ring to each half of a toggle clasp.

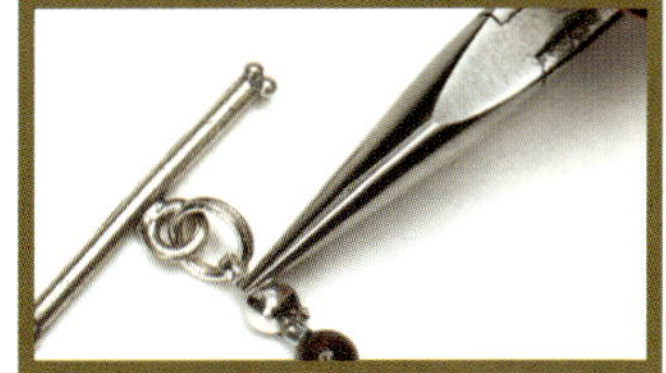

14. Use chainnose or roundnose pliers to attach each bead tip to a split ring. ✤

– Carole Rodgers
Contact Carole at rodgers@crosspaths.net.

Airy crystal necklace and earrings

Make a lightweight silver and crystal necklace with matching earrings. This tiny beading chain mimics an illusion style and is a quick alternative to stringing liquid silver. Be adventurous with the earrings—this chain is the perfect medium for long and lean shoulder-duster dangles.

necklace • 1. Determine the finished length of your necklace. (The shortest strand of this one is 16 in./41cm.) Cut a piece of beading chain to that length. Cut two more, each 2 in. (5cm) longer than the previous.

String a micro crimp, one to three crystals, and a micro crimp on the shortest strand. Continue stringing sets of crystals and micro crimps.

2. Space each grouping as desired and flatten each crimp bead (Basics, p. 3).

3. Plan your second strand by staggering the placement of the crystals in comparison with the first strand. Flatten the crimp beads. Repeat for the third strand.

4. Slide a crimp-end loop onto one end of one chain. Flatten the middle crimp section with chainnose pliers. Repeat on both ends of each piece of chain.

5. Open a jump ring (Basics) and slide on the clasp and three crimp-end loops. Close the jump ring. Repeat on the other end with just the crimp ends.

SupplyList

necklace

- 5 ft. (1.5m) beading chain, 0.6mm (Fire Mountain Gems, 800-355-2137, firemountaingems.com)
- **4** or more 10mm bicone crystals
- **33** or more 6mm bicone crystals, two colors
- **11** or more 6mm round crystals
- **50** or more micro crimps
- **6** crimp ends (loop style), 0.8mm (Fire Mountain Gems)
- **2** 4-5mm jump rings
- lobster claw clasp with jump ring
- chainnose pliers
- diagonal wire cutters

earrings

- 3 in. (76mm) or more beading chain, 0.6mm
- crystals left over from necklace
- **2** crimp ends (loop style), 0.8mm
- **2** micro crimps
- pair of earring wires
- chainnose pliers
- diagonal wire cutters

earrings • 1. Determine the finished length of your earrings. (These are 1½ in./3.8cm.) Cut a piece of beading chain to that length. String a micro crimp. Flatten the crimp bead at the end of the chain.

2. String crystals as desired.

3. Slide a crimp-end loop onto the other end of the chain. Flatten the middle section with chainnose pliers.

4. Open the end of an earring wire and slide on the crimp-end loop. Close the earring wire. Make a second earring to match the first. ✤

– *Karin Buckingham*
Contact Karin in care of BeadStyle.

Shapely hoops

Post earring findings are commonly used to dangle a beaded head pin. Here's a different technique using beading wire. This method not only gives you the freedom to vary the earring's diameter and combine beads of various shapes and sizes, but also keeps the ear nut conveniently attached.

– Don E. Wolford
Contact Don at jewelry731@yahoo.com.

1. For an earring with a 1½ in. (3.8cm) diameter, cut a 5½ in. (14cm) piece of beading wire. String a crimp bead, a 3mm round bead, and an earring post's loop. Go back through the beads just strung and make a flattened crimp (Basics, p. 3).

2. String an 8mm round bead over the crimp. String a 3mm round, a curved tube, and a 3mm round.

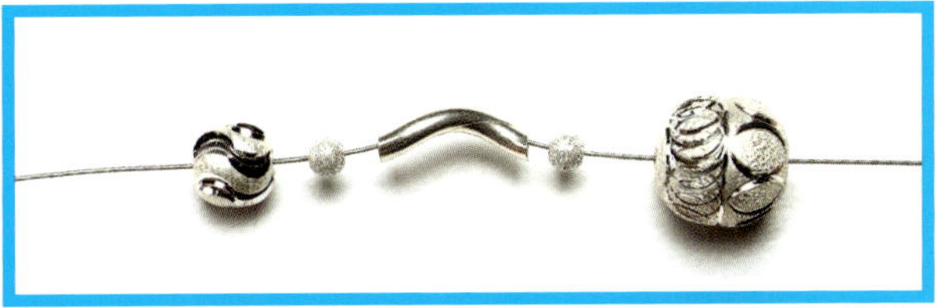

3. String a 6mm round, a 3mm round, a tube, a 3mm round, and a 10mm round.

Start with a 3mm round, and reverse the pattern in step 3, then step 2. End with an 8mm round bead.

4. String a 3mm round bead, a crimp bead, a 2mm round bead, and an ear nut. Go back through the beads just strung, tighten the wire, flatten the crimp bead, and trim the excess wire. Make a second earring to match the first. ✤

Supply List

- **2** 10mm round beads
- **4** 8mm round large-hole beads
- **4** 6mm round beads
- **20** 3mm round beads
- **2** 2mm round beads
- **8** 12mm curved tube beads (Rio Grande, 800-545-6566)
- **2** 1mm crimp beads
- pair of 4mm ball post earrings with loops
- pair of ear nuts
- flexible beading wire, .014 or .015
- chainnose pliers
- diagonal wire cutters

Color wave lariat

Color undulates through this long, flowing lariat. This necklace may appear daunting, but you'll find your rhythm quickly and string it with ease. Create the color gradation by stringing a pattern, then repeating it in reverse—like a wave that crests and retreats. Each strand follows the same pattern, but because seed beads vary in size, subtle color differences appear from strand to strand and add to the effect.

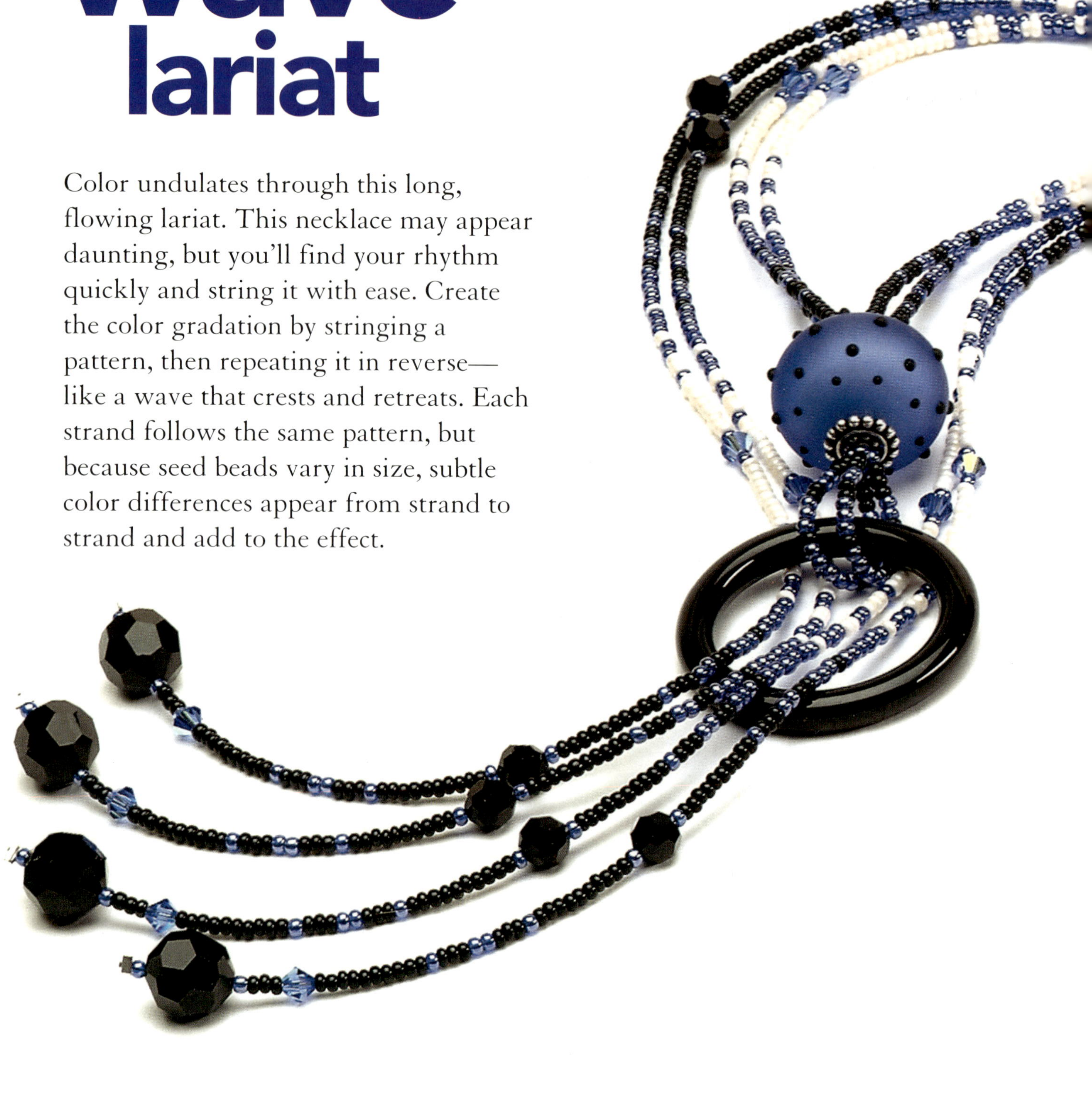

Black base-metal crimps look great with this necklace. However, they can be fragile. For more security, use a sterling silver micro crimp at the end of each tassel.

1. This necklace is worn with the art bead and ring in the center; the two long ends wrap around your neck and dangle back through the ring.

Cut two 60-in. (1.5m) pieces of beading wire.

2. String seed beads on each wire in the following pattern: one medium, three dark, two medium, two dark, three medium, one dark, five medium, one dark, three medium, two dark, two medium, three dark, and one medium. Center these beads on the wires.

3. Loop the beaded center sections around the ring.

4. String all four ends through a spacer, the art bead, and a spacer.

5. On one strand, string one medium, ten dark, one medium, three dark, two medium, two dark, three medium, one dark, six medium, one light, three medium, two light, two medium, three light, one medium, ten light, and one medium.

6. String a bicone crystal.

7. String the pattern in step 5 in reverse.

8. String a 6mm crystal. Repeat steps 5 through 8 three times.

9. String one medium, ten dark, one medium, three dark, two medium, three dark, one medium, ten dark, a bicone, three dark, and one medium.

10. String a 10mm crystal, a medium seed bead, and a crimp bead. Flatten the crimp bead (Basics, p. 3) and trim the excess wire.

Repeat steps 5 through 10 on the remaining three strands.✣

Supply List

- 15 x 20mm "poppy seed" art bead, (Joanne Morash, Blue Iris Designs, 800-431-4747, blueirisdesigns.com)
- 35mm glass ring (Eclectica, 262-641-0910)
- **24** 4mm bicone crystals
- **16** 6mm round or cube-shaped crystals
- **4** 10mm round or cube-shaped crystals
- **2** flat spacers, 8mm or smaller
- 10g size 11º seed beads, dark color
- 10g size 11º seed beads, medium color
- 10g size 11º seed beads, light color
- **4** micro crimp beads
- flexible beading wire, .014 or .015
- chainnose pliers
- diagonal wire cutters

– Nancy Kugel
Nancy offers kits for this project. Contact her at EnGee-Kay Designs, LLC, engeekay@sbcglobal.net, or engee-kay.com.